HAVERING SIXTH FORM
COLLEGE LIBRARY

Selected Poems

D0784798

WITHDRAWN FROM HAVERING COLLEGES
SIXTH FORM LIBRARY

ELIZABETH JENNINGS

Selected Poems

Copyright © Elizabeth Jennings 1979, 1985

ISBN 0 85635 282 9

All rights reserved.

First published in 1979. Second impression in 1985 by

First published in 1992 by
Carcanet Press Limited
Conavon Court
12-16 Blackfriars Street
Manchester M3 5BQ

The publisher acknowledges financial assistance from
the Arts Council of Great Britain.

Printed in England by SRP Ltd., Exeter

CONTENTS

The poems in this book follow the chronology of publication of Elizabeth Jennings's work and are taken from the *Collected Poems, The Animals' Arrival, Relationships* and *Lucidities*.

6]

8]

DELAY

The radiance of that star that leans on me
Was shining years ago. The light that now
Glitters up there my eye may never see,
And so the time lag teases me with how

Love that loves now may not reach me until
Its first desire is spent. The star's impulse
Must wait for eyes to claim it beautiful
And love arrived may find us somewhere else.

WINTER LOVE

Let us have winter loving that the heart
May be in peace and ready to partake
Of the slow pleasure spring would wish to hurry
Or that in summer harshly would awake,
And let us fall apart, O gladly weary,
The white skin shaken like a white snowflake.

REMINISCENCE

When I was happy alone, too young for love
Or to be loved in any but a way
Cloudless and gentle, I would find the day
Long as I wished its length or web to weave.

I did not know or could not know enough
To fret at thought or even try to whittle
A pattern from the shapeless stony stuff
That now confuses since I've grown too subtle.

I used the senses, did not seek to find
Something they could not touch, made numb with fear;
I felt the glittering landscape in the mind
And O was happy not to have it clear.

FANTASY

Tree without leaf I stand
Bird unfeathered cannot fly
I a beggar weep and cry
Not for coins but for a hand

To beg with. All my leaves are down,
Feathers flown and hand wrenched off
Bird and tree and beggar grown
Nothing on account of love.

ITALIAN LIGHT

It is not quite a house without the sun
And sun is what we notice, wonder at
As if stone left its hard and quarried state
To be reciprocal to light and let
The falling beams bound and rebound upon
Shutter and wall, each with assurance thrown.

So on descending from the snow we meet
Not warmth of south but houses which contrive
To be designed of sun. The builders have
Instructed hands to know where shadows fall
And made of buildings an obedient stone
Linked to the sun as waters to the moon.

AFTERNOON IN FLORENCE

This afternoon disturbs within the mind
No other afternoon, is out of time
Yet lies within a definite sun to end
In night that is in time. Yet hold it here
Our eyes, our minds, to make the city clear.

Light detains no prisoner here at all
In brick or stone but sends a freedom out
Extends a shadow like a deeper thought,
Makes churches move, once still,
Rocking in light as music rocks the bell,

So eyes make room for light and minds make room
For image of the city tangible.
We look down on the city and a dream
Opens to wakefulness, and waking on
This peace perpetuates this afternoon.

IDENTITY

When I decide I shall assemble you
Or, more precisely, when I decide which thoughts
Of mine about you fit most easily together,
Then I can learn what I have loved, what lets
Light through the mind. The residue
Of what you may be goes. I gather

Only as lovers or friends gather at all
For making friends means this—
Image and passion combined into a whole
Pattern within the loving mind, not her or his
Concurring there. You can project the full
Picture of lover or friend that is not either.

So then assemble me,
Your exact picture firm and credible,
Though as I think myself I may be free
And accurate enough.
That you love what is truthful to your will
Is all that ever can be answered for
And, what is more,
Is all we make each other when we love.

THE IDLER

An idler holds that rose as always rose,
Will not, before the bud discloses it
Within a later season, in his thought
Unwrap the flower and force the petals open
And wish in mind a different rose to happen.

So will not colour it with his own shadow
As we contrive, living beyond the present,
To move all things away from their own moment
And state another time for us. O who
Watches may yet make time refuse to grow.

So has his subtle power wiser than ours
And need elaborate no peace at all.
Watch how a landscape kindest is to idlers
Helping their shiftlessness grow to new powers,
Composing stillness round their careless will.

BELL-RINGER

The bells renew the town, discover it
And give it back itself again, the man
Pulling the rope collects the houses as
Thoughts gather in the mind unscanned, he is
Crowding the town together from the night
And making bells the morning, in remote

Control of every life (for bells shout 'Wake'
And shake out dreams, though it is he who pulls
The sleep aside). But not into his thought
Do men continue as in lives of power;

For when each bell is pulled sufficiently
He never sees himself as any cause
Or need; the sounds had left his hands to sing
A meaning for each listening separately,
A separate meaning for the single choice.

Yet bells retire to silence, need him when
Time must be shown a lucid interval
And men look up as if the air were full
Of birds descending, bells exclaiming in
His hands but shouting wider than his will.

THE CLIMBERS

To the cold peak without their careful women
(Who watching children climbing into dreams
Go dispossessed at home). The mountain moves
Away at every climb and steps are hard
Frozen along the glacier. Every man
Tied to the rope constructs himself alone.

And not the summit reached nor any pole
Touched is the wished embrace, but still to move
And as the mountain climbs to see it whole
And each mind's landscape growing more complete
As sinews strain and all the muscles knot.

One at the peak is small. His disappointment
The coloured flag flown at the lonely top,
And all the valley's motive grown obscure.
He envies the large toilers halfway there
Who still possess the mountain by desire
And, not arriving, dream in no resentment.

FISHERMEN

This to be peace, they think beside the river
Being adapted well to expectation
And their wives' mutiny at no achievement,
And yet can sit watching the promises
Escape through weeds and make a trial of biting,
Can lose them, thankful that it is not yet
Time to draw in the line and drain the net.

Learning themselves in this uncertainty
Each hardly cares whether a fish is caught,
For here is privacy, each warns himself,
The fish, inquiries in the river, not
When drawn out promises at all
Being so solid on the bank and still.

Only the boys who live in certainty,
With expectation other than the stream,
Jeer at the patience and draw up their net
Of future frogs, the river vague to them
Until it's emptied. But the old men fill
Their eyes with water, leave the river full.

THE ISLAND

All travellers escape the mainland here.
The same geology torn from the stretch
Of hostile homelands is a head of calm,
And the same sea that pounds a foreign beach
Turns strangers here familiar, looses them
Kindly as pebbles shuffled up the shore.

Each brings an island in his heart to square
With what he finds, and all is something strange
But most expected. In this innocent air
Thoughts can assume a meaning, island strength
Is outward, inward, each man measures it,
Unrolls his happiness a shining length.

And this awareness grows upon itself,
Fastens on minds, is forward, backward, here.
The island focuses escape and free
Men on the shore are also islands, steer
Self to knowledge of self in the calm sea,
Seekers who are their own discovery.

POEM IN WINTER

Today the children begin to hope for snow
And look in the sky for auguries of it.
It is not for such omens that we wait,
Our world may not be settled by the slow
Falling of flakes to lie across our thought.

And even if the snow comes down indeed
We still shall stand behind a pane of glass
Untouched by it, and watch the children press
Their image on the drifts the snow has laid
Upon a winter they think they have made.

This is a wise illusion. Better to
Believe the near world is created by
A wish, a shaping hand, a certain eye,
Than hide in the mind's corner as we do
As though there were no world, no fall of snow.

SONG AT THE BEGINNING OF AUTUMN

Now watch this autumn that arrives
In smells. All looks like summer still;
Colours are quite unchanged, the air
On green and white serenely thrives.
Heavy the trees with growth and full
The fields. Flowers flourish everywhere.

Proust who collected time within
A child's cake would understand
The ambiguity of this—
Summer still raging while a thin
Column of smoke stirs from the land
Proving that autumn gropes for us.

But every season is a kind
Of rich nostalgia. We give names—
Autumn and summer, winter, spring—
As though to unfasten from the mind
Our moods and give them outward forms.
We want the certain, solid thing.

But I am carried back against
My will into a childhood where
Autumn is bonfires, marbles, smoke;
I lean against my window fenced
From evocations in the air.
When I said autumn, autumn broke.

KINGS

You send an image hurrying out of doors
When you depose a king and seize his throne:
You exile symbols when you take by force.

And even if you say the power's your own,
That you are your own hero, your own king
You will not wear the meaning of the crown.

The power a ruler has is how men bring
Their thoughts to bear upon him, how their minds
Construct the grandeur from the simple thing.

And kings prevented from their proper ends
Make a deep lack in men's imaginings;
Heroes are nothing without worshipping,

Will not diminish into lovers, friends.

THE ENEMIES

Last night they came across the river and
Entered the city. Women were awake
With lights and food. They entertained the band,
Not asking what the men had come to take
Or what strange tongue they spoke
Or why they came so suddenly through the land.

Now in the morning all the town is filled
With stories of the swift and dark invasion;
The women say that not one stranger told
A reason for his coming. The intrusion
Was not for devastation:
Peace is apparent still on hearth and field.

Yet all the city is a haunted place.
Man meeting man speaks cautiously. Old friends
Close up the candid looks upon their face.
There is no warmth in hands accepting hands;
Each ponders, 'Better hide myself in case
Those strangers have set up their homes in minds
I used to walk in. Better draw the blinds
Even if the strangers haunt in my own house.'

IN THIS TIME

If the myth's outworn, the legend broken,
    Useless even within the child's story
Since he sees well they now bring light no longer
    Into our eyes: and if our past retreats
And blows away like dust along the desert,
    Not leading to our moment now at all,
Settling us in this place and saying 'Here
    In you I shall continue'—then what kind
Of lives have we? Can we make myths revive
    By breathing on them? Is there any taper
That will return the glitter to our eyes?

We have retreated inward to our minds
    Too much, have made rooms there with all doors closed,
All windows shuttered. There we sit and mope
    The myth away, set by the lovely legends;
Hardly we hear the children shout outside.
    We only know a way to love ourselves,
Have lost the power that made us lose ourselves.
    O let the wind outside blow in again
And the dust come and all the children's voices.
    Let anything that is not us return.
Myths are the memories we have rejected
    And legends need the freedom of our minds.

BEYOND POSSESSION

Our images withdraw, the rose returns
To what it was before we looked at it.
We lift our looks from where the water runs
And it's pure river once again, we write
No emblems on the trees. A way begins
Of living where we have no need to beat
The petals down to get the scent of rose
Or sign our features where the water goes.

All is itself. Each man himself entire,
Not even plucking out his thought, not even
Bringing a tutored wilfulness to bear
Upon the rose, the water. Each has given
Essence of water back to itself, essence of flower,
Till he is yoked to his own heart and driven
Inward to find a private kind of peace
And not a mind reflecting his own face.

Yet must go deeper still, must move to love
Where thought is free to let the water ride,
Is liberal to the rose giving it life
And setting even its own shadow aside;
Till flower and water blend with freedom of
Passion that does not close them in and hide
Their deepest natures; but the heart is strong
To beat with rose and river in one song.

TRIBUTE

Sometimes the tall poem leans across the page
And the whole world seems near, a simple thing.
Then all the arts of mind and hand engage
To make the shadow tangible. O white
As silence is the page where words shall sing
And all the shadows be drawn into light.

And no one else is necessary then.
The poem is enough that joins me to
The world that seems too far to grasp at when
Images fail and words are gabbled speech:
At those times clarity appears in you,
Your mind holds meanings that my mind can reach.

Are you remote, then, when words play their part
With a fine arrogance within the poem?
Will the words keep all else outside my heart,
Even you, my test of life and gauge?
No, for you are that place where poems find room,
The tall abundant shadow on my page.

FOR A CHILD BORN DEAD

What ceremony can we fit
You into now? If you had come
Out of a warm and noisy room
To this, there'd be an opposite
For us to know you by. We could
Imagine you in lively mood

And then look at the other side,
The mood drawn out of you, the breath
Defeated by the power of death.
But we have never seen you stride
Ambitiously the world we know.
You could not come and yet you go.

But there is nothing now to mar
Your clear refusal of our world.
Not in our memories can we mould
You or distort your character.
Then all our consolation is
That grief can be as pure as this.

COMMUNICATION

No use to speak, no good to tell you that
A love is worn away not by the one
Who leaves but by the one who stays and hopes,
Since you would rather have the hoping still
Than be yourself again. What can I say
Who know, better than you, the one who has
Moved on, away, not loving him at all?

And certainly to you I would relinquish
This knowledge held in other ways of feeling
Though dressed up in the properties of passion
Looked at by you. Something is deeply held
By me who never deeply searched at all
And we are not yet wise enough or subtle
To offer anyone a state of mind.

This the particular problem, and I search
A power over our general condition,
Where love is like a landscape we can change
And where desire may be transformed to friendship
If friendship gives the really wanted knowledge,
Where we can see the end and have the power
To take the journey there a different way,
And we can move our minds as we move houses:
Where love is more than lucky in the land.

MIRRORS

Was it a mirror then across a room,
A crowded room of parties where the smoke
Rose to the ceiling with the talk? The glass
Stared back at me a half-familiar face
Yet something hoped for. When at last you came
It was as if the distant mirror spoke.

That loving ended as all self-love ends
And teaches us that only fair-grounds have
The right to show us halls of mirrors where
In every place we look we see our stare
Taunting our own identities. But love
Perceives without a mirror in the hands.

IN THE NIGHT

Out of my window late at night I gape
And see the stars but do not watch them really,
And hear the trains but do not listen clearly;
Inside my mind I turn about to keep
Myself awake, yet am not there entirely.
Something of me is out in the dark landscape.

How much am I then what I think, how much what I feel?
How much the eye that seems to keep stars straight?
Do I control what I can contemplate
Or is it my vision that's amenable?
I turn in my mind, my mind is a room whose wall
I can see the top of but never completely scale.

All that I love is, like the night, outside,
Good to be gazed at, looking as if it could
With a simple gesture be brought inside my head
Or in my heart. But my thoughts about it divide
Me from my object. Now deep in my bed
I turn and the world turns on the other side.

ANSWERS

I kept my answers small and kept them near;
Big questions bruised my mind but still I let
Small answers be a bulwark to my fear.

The huge abstractions I kept from the light;
Small things I handled and caressed and loved.
I let the stars assume the whole of night.

But the big answers clamoured to be moved
Into my life. Their great audacity
Shouted to be acknowledged and believed.

Even when all small answers build up to
Protection of my spirit, still I hear
Big answers striving for their overthrow

And all the great conclusions coming near.

OLD MAN

His age drawn out behind him to be watched:
It is his shadow you may say. That dark
He paints upon the wall is his past self,
A mark he only leaves when he is still
    And he is still now always,
At ease and watching all his life assemble.

And he intends nothing but watching. What
His life has made of him his shadow shows—
Fine graces gone but dignity remaining,
While all he shuffled after is composed
    Into a curve of dark, of silences:
An old man tranquil in his silences.

And we move round him, are his own world turning,
Spinning it seems to him, leaving no shadow
To blaze our trail. We are our actions only:
He is himself, abundant and assured,
    All action thrown away,
And time is slowing where his shadow stands.

TAKEN BY SURPRISE

Before, the anticipation, the walk merely
Under the oaks, (the afternoon crushed down
To his pressed footprints), noon surrendered, forgotten—
And the man moving, singular under the sun
With the hazel held in his hand lightly, lightly:
On the edge of his ear the lisp of the wind among
Untrembling leaves. Sun at the tips of the trees
Looked down, looked cold, and the man felt easy there.
His shadow seemed fitting as never before it was,
And the almost silence a space a man may enter
And be forgotten by all but his secret thoughts.
Then, something taking his fingers: 'Is it the wind?'
He thought and looked to see if the branches moved.
But nothing unusual stirred the trees, again
His fingers trembled, the hazel shook, he felt
Suddenly life in the twig as a woman feels
Abrupt and close the stir of the unborn child.
O and the afternoon was altered then;
Power from all quarters flung at him, silence broke
And deft but uneasy far at the back of his mind
A word like water shuddered, streams gushed and fountains
Rose as the hazel leapt from his mastered hand.

THE STORM

Right in the middle of the storm it was.
So many winds were blowing none could tell
Which was the fiercest or if trees that bent
So smoothly to each impulse had been waiting
All of their growing-time for just that impulse
To prove how pliable they were. Beneath,
Beasts fled away through fern, and stiffest grasses,
Which bent like fluid things, made tidal motion.

These who had never met before but in
Calmest surroundings, found all shadows mingling;
No stance could be struck here, no peace attained,
And words blew round in broken syllables,
Half-meanings sounded out like trumpet blasts,
Decisive words were driven into hiding.
Yet some hilarity united them
And faces, carved and cleared by rain and lightning,
Stared out as if they never had been seen.

And children now, lost in the wood together,
Becoming the behaviour of the wind,
The way the light fell, learnt each other newly
And sudden gentleness was apprehended
Till the abating winds, the whole storm swerving
Into another quarter, left them standing
Unwild and watching in bewilderment
Their own delusive shadows slow and part.

HER GARDEN

Not at the full moon will she pick those flowers
For sudden shade indoors would make them wilt.
The petals would drop down on polished wood
Adding another element to decay
Which all her old rooms are infected with.

Only outside she can put off the course
Of her disease. She has the garden built
Within high walls so no one can intrude.
When people pass she only hears the way
Their footsteps sound, never their closer breath.

But in her borders she observes the powers
Of bud and branch, forgetting how she felt
When, blood within her veins like sap, she stood,
Her arms like branches bare above the day
And all the petals strewn along her path.

No matter now for she has bridged the pause
Between fruition and decay. She'll halt
A little in her garden while a mood
Of peace so fills her that she cannot say
Whether it is the flowers' life or her death.

SUMMER AND TIME

Now when the days descend
We do not let them lie
But ponder on the end,
How morning air drained dry
Of mist will but contend
Later with evening sky.

And so we mix up time.
Children, we say, ignore
Before and after, chime
Only the present hour.
But we are wrong, they climb
What time is aiming for

But beg no lastingness.
And it is we who try
In every hour to press
Befores and afters, sigh
All the great hour's success
And set the spoiling by.

Heavy the heat today,
Even the clocks seem slow.
But children make no play
With summers years ago.
It is we who betray
Who tease the sun-dial so.

AT NOON

Lying upon my bed I see
Full moon at ease. Each way I look
A world established without me
Proclaims itself. I take a book
And flutter through the pages where
Sun leaps through shadows. And I stare

Straight through the words and find again
A world that has no need of me.
The poems stride against the strain
Of complex rhythms. Separately
I lie and struggle to become
More than a centre to this room.

I want the ease of noon outside
Also the strength of words which move
Against their music. All the wide
And casual day I need to stuff
With my own meaning and the book
Of poems reflect me where I look.

GHOSTS

Those houses haunt in which we leave
Something undone. It is not those
Great words or silences of love

That spread their echoes through a place
And fill the locked-up unbreathed gloom.
Ghosts do not haunt with any face

That we have known; they only come
With arrogance to thrust at us
Our own omissions in a room.

The words we would not speak they use,
The deeds we dared not act they flaunt,
Our nervous silences they bruise;

It is our helplessness they choose
And our refusals that they haunt.

ABSENCE

I visited the place where we last met.
Nothing was changed, the gardens were well-tended,
The fountains sprayed their usual steady jet;
There was no sign that anything had ended
And nothing to instruct me to forget.

The thoughtless birds that shook out of the trees,
Singing an ecstasy I could not share,
Played cunning in my thoughts. Surely in these
Pleasures there could not be a pain to bear
Or any discord shake the level breeze.

It was because the place was just the same
That made your absence seem a savage force,
For under all the gentleness there came
An earthquake tremor: fountain, birds and grass
Were shaken by my thinking of your name.

DISGUISES

Always we have believed
We can change overnight,
Put a different look on the face,
Old passions out of sight:
And find new days relieved
Of all that we regretted
But something always stays
And will not be outwitted.

Say we put on dark glasses,
Wear different clothes and walk
With a new unpractised stride—
Always somebody passes
Undeceived by disguises
Or the different way we talk.
And we who could have defied
Anything if it was strange
Have nowhere we can hide
From those who refuse to change.

THE PARTING

Though there was nothing final then,
No word or look or sign,
I felt some ending in the air
As when a sensed design
Draws back from the completing touch
And dies along a line.

For through the words that seemed to show
That we were learning each
Trick of the other's thought and sense,
A shyness seemed to reach
As if such talk continuing
Would make the hour too rich.

Maybe this strangeness only was
The safe place all men make
To hide themselves from happiness;
I only know I lack
The strangeness our last meeting had
And try to force it back.

RESEMBLANCES

Always I look for some reminding feature,
Compel a likeness where there is not one,
As in a gallery I trace the stature
Of that one's boldness or of this one's grace.
Yet likenesses so searched for will yield none;
One feature, yes, but never the whole face.

So every face falls back into its parts
And once-known glances leave the candid look
Of total strangeness. Where the likeness starts
We fix attention, set aside the rest,
As those who scan for notes a thick-packed book,
Recalling only what has pleased them best.

And doing this, so often I have missed
Some recognition never known before,
Some knowledge which I never could have guessed.
And how if all the others whom I pass
Should like myself be always searching for
The special features only one face has?

Always the dear enchanted moment stays.
We cannot unlearn all whom we have loved;
Who can tear off like calendars the days
Or wipe out features fixed within the mind?
Only there should be some way to be moved
Beyond the likeness to the look behind.

A DEATH

'His face shone' she said,
'Three days I had him in my house,
Three days before they took him from his bed,
And never have I felt so close.'

'Always alive he was
A little drawn away from me.
Looks are opaque when living and his face
Seemed hiding something, carefully.'

'But those three days before
They took his body out, I used to go
And talk to him. That shining from him bore
No secrets. Living, he never looked or answered so.'

Sceptic, I listened, then
Noted what peace she seemed to have,
How tenderly she put flowers on his grave
But not as if he might return again
Or shine or seem quite close:
Rather to please us were the flowers she gave.

THE SHOT

The bullet shot me and I lay
So calm beneath the sun, the trees
Shook out their shadows in the breeze
Which carried half the sky away.

I did not know if I was dead,
A feeling close to sleep lay near
Yet through it I could see the clear
River and grass as if in bed

I lay and watched the morning come
Gentle behind the blowing stuff
Of curtains. But the pain was rough,
Not fitting to a sunlit room.

And I am dying, then, I thought.
I felt them lift me up and take
What seemed my body. Should I wake
And stop the darkness in my throat

And break the mist before my eyes?
I felt the bullet's leaps and swerves.
And none is loved as he deserves
And death is a disguise.

SONG FOR A DEPARTURE

Could you indeed come lightly
Leaving no mark at all
Even of footsteps, briefly
Visit not change the air
Of this or the other room,
Have quick words with us yet be
Calm and unhurried here?

So that we should not need—
When you departed lightly
Even as swift as coming
Letting no shadow fall—
Changes, surrenders, fear,
Speeches grave to the last,
But feel no loss at all?

Lightest things in the mind
Go deep at last and can never
Be planned or weighed or lightly
Considered or set apart.
Then come like a great procession,
Touch hours with drums and flutes:
Fill all the rooms of our houses
And haunt them when you depart.

CHOICES

Inside the room I see the table laid,
Four chairs, a patch of light the lamp has made

And people there so deep in tenderness
They could not speak a word of happiness.

Outside I stand and see my shadow drawn
Lengthening the clipped grass of the cared-for lawn.

Above, their roof holds half the sky behind.
A dog barks bringing distances to mind.

Comfort, I think, or safety then, or both?
I warm the cold air with my steady breath.

They have designed a way to live and I,
Clothed in confusion, set their choices by:

Though sometimes one looks up and sees me there,
Alerts his shadow, pushes back his chair

And, opening windows wide, looks out at me
And close past words we stare. It seems that he

Urges my darkness, dares it to be freed
Into that room. We need each other's need.

TELLING STORIES

For M.

Telling you stories I forget that you
Already know the end
And I forget that I am building up
A world in which no piece must be put back
In the wrong place or time
Else you will make me go back to the start.

My scope for improvising will not ever
Deceive you into taking
A change of plan. You are so grounded in
Your absolutes, even the worlds we build
Of thin thoughts, lean ideas
You will not let us alter but expect

The thing repeated whole. Is this then what
We call your innocence—
This fine decision not to have things changed?
Is this your way of stopping clocks, of damming
The thrusting stream of time?
Has a repeated story so much power?

Such is the trust you have not in large things
But in the placing of
A verb, an adjective, a happy end.
The stories that we tell, we tell against
Ourselves then at the last
Since all the worlds we make we stand outside

Leaning on time and swayed about by it
While you stand firm within the fragile plot.

A FEAR

Always to keep it in and never spare
Even a hint of pain, go guessing on,
Feigning a sacrifice, forging a tear
For someone else's grief, but still to bear
Inward the agony of self alone—

And all the masks I carry on my face,
The smile for you, the grave considered air
For you and for another some calm grace
When still within I carry an old fear
A child could never speak about, disgrace
That no confession could assuage or clear.

But once within a long and broken night
I woke and threw the shutters back for air
(The sudden moths were climbing to the light)
And from another window I saw stare
A face like mine still dream-bereft and white
And, like mine, shaken by a child's nightmare.

IN A FOREIGN CITY

You cannot speak for no one knows
Your language. You must try to catch
By glances or a steadfast gaze
The attitude of those you watch.
No conversations can amaze:
Noises may find you but not speech.

Now you have circled silence, stare
With all the subtlety of sight.
Noise may trap ears but eye discerns
How someone on his elbow turns
And in the moon's long exile here
Touches another in the night.

THE ROMAN FORUM

Look at the Forum
Commanded now by Roman pines:
Walk down the ancient paths
Rubbed smooth by footprints in the past and now
Broken among the baths
And battered columns where the lizards go
In zig-zag movements like the lines
Of this decorum.

Not what the man
Who carved the column, reared the arch
Or shaped the building meant
Is what we marvel at. Perfection here
Is quite within our reach,
These ruins now are more than monument.
See how the houses disappear
Into a plan

Connived at by
Shadows of trees or light approved
By sun and not designed
By architects. Three columns eased away
From all support are moved
By how the shadows shake them from behind.
The pine trees droop their dark and sway
Swifter than eye

Can catch them all,
O and the heart is drawn to sense,
Eye and the mind are one.
The fragments here of former markets make
(Preserved by the intense
Glare of the Roman unremitting sun),
Such cities that the heart would break
And shadows fall

To see them pass.
Removed from Rome you, half-asleep,
Observe the shadows stray.
Above, the pines are playing with the light,
Dream now so dark and deep
That when you wake those columns, lucid, free,
Will burst like flowers into white
Springing from grass.

A CONVERSATION IN THE GARDENS OF
THE VILLA CELIMONTANA, ROME

For A.

Deeper the shadows underneath the pines
Than their own trunks and roots. Under the hard
Blue of the sky (a Roman blue, they say)
I watched the afternoon weave its designs
Lucid as crystal on this first June day.

The fountains softly displayed themselves. The grass,
Unpressed by footprints yet, looked cool and young;
Over the paths we saw our shadows pass
And in the air the glittering moments strung
Together like a brilliance under glass.

Suddenly to this fullness our words went
Talking of visionaries, of those men
Who make a stillness deeper than an act,
Who probe beyond a place where passion's spent
And apprehend by purest intellect.

You talked of this and in between your words
I sensed (still shadowed by my own warm flesh)
That you had known such apprehensions and
Back in the garden where the pine-trees stand
Held to that moment where all hungers hush.

Yes but the garden held a stillness too.
My mind could seize upon the pleasures there,
Yet in between the fountains and the grass,
The leaning pines, the overriding air,
I glimpsed a radiance where no shadows pass.

A ROMAN WINDOW

After the griefs of night,
Over the doors of day,
Here by this window-sill
I watch the climbing light
As early footsteps steal
Enormous shadows away.

Tenderly from this height
I feel compassion come—
People pestered by hours,
The morning swung to sight
As all the city stirs
And trembles in my room.

So from a stance of calm,
A stepping out of sleep,
My shadow once again
Disperses in the warm
Day with its lives more deep
Than any pleasure or pain.

FOUNTAIN

Let it disturb no more at first
Than the hint of a pool predicted far in a forest,
Or a sea so far away that you have to open
Your window to hear it.
Think of it then as elemental, as being
Necessity,
Not for a cup to be taken to it and not
For lips to linger or eye to receive itself
Back in reflection, simply
As water the patient moon persuades and stirs.

And then step closer,
Imagine rivers you might indeed embark on,
Waterfalls where you could
Silence an afternoon by staring but never
See the same tumult twice.
Yes come out of the narrow street and enter
The full piazza. Come where the noise compels.
Statues are bowing down to the breaking air.

Observe it there—the fountain, too fast for shadows,
Too wild for the lights which illuminate it to hold,
Even a moment, an ounce of water back;
Stare at such prodigality and consider
It is the elegance here, it is the taming,
The keeping fast in a thousand flowering sprays,
That builds this energy up but lets the watchers
See in that stress an image of utter calm,
A stillness there. It is how we must have felt
Once at the edge of some perpetual stream,
Fearful of touching, bringing no thirst at all,
Panicked by no perception of ourselves
But drawing the water down to the deepest wonder.

SAN PAOLO FUORI LE MURA, ROME

It is the stone makes stillness here, I think
There could not be so much of silence if
The columns were not set there rank on rank,
For silence needs a shape in which to sink
And stillness needs these shadows for its life.

My darkness throws so little space before
My body where it stands, and yet my mind
Needs the large echoing churches and the roar
Of streets outside its own calm place to find
Where the soft doves of peace withdraw, withdraw.

The alabaster windows here permit
Only suggestions of the sun to slide
Into the church and make a glow in it;
The battering daylight leaps at large outside
Though what slips here through jewels seems most fit.

And here one might in his discovered calm
Feel the great building draw away from him,
His head bent closely down upon his arm,
With all the sun subsiding to a dim
Past-dreamt-of peace, a kind of coming home.

For me the senses still have their full sway
Even where prayer comes quicker than an act.
I cannot quite forget the blazing day,
The alabaster windows or the way
The light refuses to be called abstract.

LETTER FROM ASSISI

Here you will find peace, they said,
Here where silence is so wide you hear it,
Where every church you enter is a kind
Continuing of thought,
Here there is ease.
Now on this road, looking up to the hill
Where the town looks severe and seems to say
There is no softness here, no sensual joy,
Close by the flowers that fling me back to England—
The bleeding poppy and the dusty vetch
And all blue flowers reflecting back the sky—
It is not peace I feel but some nostalgia,
So that a hand which draws a shutter back,
An eye which warms as it observes a child,
Hurt me with homesickness. Peace pales and withers.

The doves demur, an English voice divides
The distances. It is the afternoon,
But here siesta has no place because
All of the day is strung with silences.
Bells wound the air and I remember one
Who long ago confided how such ringing
Brought salt into their mouth, tears to their eyes.
I think I understand a mood like that:
Doves, bells, the silent hills, O all the trappings
We dress our plans of peace in, fail me now.
I search some shadow wider than my own,
Some apprehension which requires no mood
Of local silence or a sense of prayer—
An open glance that looks from some high window
And illustrates a need I wish to share.

THE ANNUNCIATION

Nothing will ease the pain to come
Though now she sits in ecstasy
And lets it have its way with her.
The angel's shadow in the room
Is lightly lifted as if he
Had never terrified her there.

The furniture again returns
To its old simple state. She can
Take comfort from the things she knows
Though in her heart new loving burns
Something she never gave to man
Or god before, and this god grows

Most like a man. She wonders how
To pray at all, what thanks to give
And whom to give them to. 'Alone
To all men's eyes I now must go'
She thinks, 'And by myself must live
With a strange child that is my own.'

So from her ecstasy she moves
And turns to human things at last
(Announcing angels set aside).
It is a human child she loves
Though a god stirs beneath her breast
And great salvations grip her side.

TERESA OF AVILA

Spain. The wild dust, the whipped corn, earth easy for footsteps, shallow to starving seeds. High sky at night like walls. Silences surrounding Avila.

She, teased by questions, aching for reassurance. Calm in confession before incredulous priests. Then back—to the pure illumination, the profound personal prayer, the four waters.

Water from the well first, drawn up painfully. Clinking of pails. Dry lips at the well-head. Parched grass bending. And the dry heart too—waiting for prayer.

Then the water-wheel, turning smoothly. Somebody helping unseen. A keen hand put out, gently sliding the wheel. Then water and the aghast spirit refreshed and quenched.

Not this only. Other waters also, clear from a spring or a pool. Pouring from a fountain like child's play—but the child is elsewhere. And she, kneeling, cooling her spirit at the water, comes nearer, nearer.

Then the entire cleansing, utterly from nowhere. No wind ruffled it, no shadows slid across it. Her mind met it, her will approved. And all beyonds, backwaters, dry words of old prayers were lost in it. The water was only itself.

And she knelt there, waited for the shadows to cross the light which the water made, waited for familiar childhood illuminations (the lamp by the bed, the candle in church, sun beckoned by horizons)—but this light was none of these, was only how the water looked, how the will turned and was still. Even the image of light itself withdrew, and the dry dust on the winds of Spain outside her halted. Moments spread not into hours but stood still. No dove brought the tokens of peace. She was the peace that her prayers had promised. And the silences suffered no shadows.

SONG FOR A BIRTH OR A DEATH

Last night I saw the savage world
And heard the blood beat up the stair;
The fox's bark, the owl's shrewd pounce,
The crying creatures—all were there,
And men in bed with love and fear.

The slit moon only emphasised
How blood must flow and teeth must grip.
What does the calm light understand,
The light which draws the tide and ship
And drags the owl upon its prey
And human creatures lip to lip?

Last night I watched how pleasure must
Leap from disaster with its will:
The fox's fear, the watch-dog's lust
Know that all matings mean a kill:
And human creatures kissed in trust
Feel the blood throb to death until

The seed is struck, the pleasure's done,
The birds are thronging in the air;
The moon gives way to widespread sun.
Yes but the pain still crouches where
The young fox and the child are trapped
And cries of love are cries of fear.

FAMILY AFFAIRS

No longer here the blaze that we'd engender
Out of pure wrath. We pick at quarrels now
As fussy women stitch at cotton, slow
Now to forget and too far to surrender.
The anger stops, apologies also.

And in this end of summer, weighted calm
(Climate of mind, I mean), we are apart
Further than ever when we wished most harm.
Indifference lays a cold hand on the heart;
We need the violence to keep us warm.

Have we then learnt at last how to untie
The bond of birth, umbilical long cord,
So that we live quite unconnected by
The blood we share? What monstrous kind of sword
Can sever veins and still we do not die?

A GAME OF CHESS

The quiet moves, the gently shaded room:
It is like childhood once again when I
Sat with a tray of toys and you would come
To take my temperature and make me lie
Under the clothes and sleep. Now peacefully

We sit above the intellectual game.
Pure mathematics seems to rule the board
Emotionless. And yet I feel the same
As when I sat and played without a word
Inventing kingdoms where great feelings stirred.

Is it that knight and king and small squat castle
Store up emotion, bring it under rule,
So that the problems now with which we wrestle
Seem simply of the mind? Do feelings cool
Beneath the order of an abstract school?

Never entirely, since the whole thing brings
Me back to childhood when I was distressed:
You seem the same who put away my things
At night, my toys and tools of childish lust.
My king is caught now in a world of trust.

MY GRANDMOTHER

She kept an antique shop—or it kept her.
Among Apostle spoons and Bristol glass,
The faded silks, the heavy furniture,
She watched her own reflection in the brass
Salvers and silver bowls, as if to prove
Polish was all, there was no need of love.

And I remember how I once refused
To go out with her, since I was afraid.
It was perhaps a wish not to be used
Like antique objects. Though she never said
That she was hurt, I still could feel the guilt
Of that refusal, guessing how she felt.

Later, too frail to keep a shop, she put
All her best things in one long narrow room.
The place smelt old, of things too long kept shut,
The smell of absences where shadows come
That can't be polished. There was nothing then
To give her own reflection back again.

And when she died I felt no grief at all,
Only the guilt of what I once refused.
I walked into her room among the tall
Sideboards and cupboards—things she never used
But needed; and no finger-marks were there,
Only the new dust falling through the air.

IN PRAISE OF CREATION

That one bird, one star,
The one flash of the tiger's eye
Purely assert what they are,
Without ceremony testify.

Testify to order, to rule—
How the birds mate at one time only,
How the sky is, for a certain time, full
Of birds, the moon sometimes cut thinly.

And the tiger trapped in the cage of his skin,
Watchful over creation, rests
For the blood to pound, the drums to begin,
Till the tigress' shadow casts

A darkness over him, a passion, a scent,
The world goes turning, turning, the season
Sieves earth to its one sure element
And the blood beats beyond reason.

Then quiet, and birds folding their wings,
The new moon waiting for years to be stared at here,
The season sinks to satisfied things—
Man with his mind ajar.

WORLD I HAVE NOT MADE

I have sometimes thought how it would have been
if I had had to create the whole thing myself—
my life certainly but also something else;
I mean a world which I could inhabit freely,
ideas, objects, everything prepared;
not ideas simply as Plato knew them,
shadows of shadows, but more like furniture,
something to move around and live in,
something I had made. But still there would be
all that I hadn't made—animals, stars,
tides tugging against me, moon uncaring,
and the trying to love without reciprocity.
All this is here still. It is hard, hard,
even with free faith outlooking boundaries,
to come to terms with obvious suffering.
I live in a world I have not created
inward or outward. There is a sweetness
in willing surrender: I trail my ideas
behind great truths. My ideas are like shadows
and sometimes I consider how it would have been
to create a credo, objects, ideas
and then to live with them. I can understand
when tides most tug and the moon is remote
and the trapped wild beast is one with its shadow,
how even great faith leaves room for abysses
and the taut mind turns to its own requirings.

HARVEST AND CONSECRATION

After the heaped piles and the cornsheaves waiting
To be collected, gathered into barns,
After all fruits have burst their skins, the sating
    Season cools and turns,
And then I think of something that you said
Of when you held the chalice and the bread.

I spoke of Mass and thought of it as close
To how a season feels which stirs and brings
Fire to the hearth, food to the hungry house
    And strange, uncovered things—
God in a garden then in sheaves of corn
And the white bread a way to be reborn.

I thought of priest as midwife and as mother
Feeling the pain, feeling the pleasure too,
    All opposites together,
Until you said no one could feel such passion
And still preserve the power of consecration.

And it is true. How cool the gold sheaves lie,
Rich without need to ask for any more
Richness. The seed, the simple thing must die
    If only to restore
Our faith in fruitful, hidden things. I see
The wine and bread protect our ecstasy.

A WORLD OF LIGHT

Yes when the dark withdrew I suffered light
And saw the candles heave beneath the wax,
I watched the shadow of my old self dwindle
As softly on my recollection stole
A mood the senses could not touch or damage,
A sense of peace beyond the breathing word.

Day dawdled at my elbow. It was night
Within. I saw my hands, their soft dark backs
Keeping me from the noise outside. The candle
Seemed snuffed into a deep and silent pool:
It drew no shadow round my constant image
For in a dazzling dark my spirit stirred.

But still I questioned it. My inward sight
Still knew the senses and the senses' tracks,
I felt my flesh and clothes, a rubbing sandal,
And distant voices wishing to console.
My mind was keen to understand and rummage
To find assurance in the sounds I heard.

Then senses ceased and thoughts were driven quite
Away (no act of mine). I could relax
And feel a fire no earnest prayer can kindle;
Old parts of peace dissolved into a whole
And like a bright thing proud in its new plumage
My mind was keen as an attentive bird.

Yes, fire, light, air, birds, wax, the sun's own height
I draw from now, but every image breaks.
Only a child's simplicity can handle
Such moments when the hottest fire feels cool,
And every breath is like a sudden homage
To peace that penetrates and is not feared.

A REQUIEM

It is the ritual not the fact
That brings a held emotion to
Its breaking-point. This man I knew
Only a little, by his death
Shows me a love I thought I lacked
And all the stirrings underneath.

It is the calm, the solemn thing,
Not the distracted mourner's cry
Or the cold place where dead things lie,
That teaches me I cannot claim
To stand aside. These tears which sting—
Are they from sorrow or from shame?

THE RESURRECTION

I was the one who waited in the garden
Doubting the morning and the early light.
I watched the mist lift off its own soft burden,
Permitting not believing my own sight.

If there were sudden noises I dismissed
Them as a trick of sound, a sleight of hand.
Not by a natural joy could I be blessed
Or trust a thing I could not understand.

Maybe I was a shadow thrown by some
Who, weeping, came to lift away the stone,
Or was I but the path on which the sun,
Too heavy for itself, was loosed and thrown?

I heard the voices and the recognition
And love like kisses heard behind the walls.
Were they my tears which fell, a real contrition?
Or simply April with its waterfalls?

It was by negatives I learnt my place.
The garden went on growing and I sensed
A sudden breeze that blew across my face.
Despair returned but now it danced, it danced.

MANTEGNA'S AGONY IN THE GARDEN

The agony is formal; three
Bodies are stretched in pure repose,
One's halo leans against a tree,
Over a book his fingers close:
One's arms are folded carefully.

The third man lies with sandalled feet
Thrust in the path. They almost touch
Three playful rabbits. Down the street,
Judas and his procession march
Making the distance seem discreet.

Even the praying figure has
A cared-for attitude. This art
Puts down the city and the mass
Of mountains like a counterpart
Of pain disguised as gentleness.

And yet such careful placing here
Of mountain, men and agony,
Being so solid makes more clear
The pain. Pain is particular.
The foreground shows a barren tree:
Is it a vulture crouching there,
No symbol but a prophecy?

VISIT TO AN ARTIST

For David Jones

Window upon the wall, a balcony
With a light chair, the air and water so
Mingled you could not say which was the sun
And which the adamant yet tranquil spray.
But nothing was confused and nothing slow:
Each way you looked, always the sea, the sea.

And every shyness that we brought with us
Was drawn into the pictures on the walls.
It was so good to sit quite still and lose
Necessity of discourse, words to choose
And wonder which were honest and which false.

Then I remembered words that you had said
Of art as gesture and as sacrament,
A mountain under the calm form of paint
Much like the Presence under wine and bread—
Art with its largesse and its own restraint.

LAZARUS

It was the amazing white, it was the way he simply
Refused to answer our questions, it was the cold pale glance
Of death upon him, the smell of death that truly
Declared his rising to us. It was no chance
Happening, as a man may fill a silence
Between two heart-beats, seem to be dead and then
Astonish us with the closeness of his presence;
This man was dead, I say it again and again.
All of our sweating bodies moved towards him
And our minds moved too, hungry for finished faith.
He would not enter our world at once with words
That we might be tempted to twist or argue with:
Cold like a white root pressed in the bowels of earth
He looked, but also vulnerable—like birth.

THE DIAMOND CUTTER

Not what the light will do but how he shapes it
And what particular colours it will bear,

And something of the climber's concentration
Seeing the white peak, setting the right foot there.

Not how the sun was plausible at morning
Nor how it was distributed at noon,

And not how much the single stone could show
But rather how much brilliance it would shun;

Simply a paring down, a cleaving to
One object, as the star-gazer who sees

One single comet polished by its fall
Rather than countless, untouched galaxies.

STARGAZERS AND OTHERS

One, staring out stars,
Lost himself in looking and almost
Forgot glass, eye, air, space;
Simply, he thought, the world is improved
By my staring, how the still glass leaps
When the sky thuds in like tides.

Another, making love, once
Stared so far over his pleasure
That woman, world, the spiral
Of taut bodies, the clinging hands, broke apart
And he saw, as the stargazer sees,
Landscapes made to be looked at,
Fruit to fall, not be plucked.

In you also something
Of such vision occurs.
How else would I have learnt
The tapered stars, the pause
On the nervous spiral? Names I need
Stronger than love, desire,
Passion, pleasure. O discover
Some star and christen it, but let me be
The space that your eye moves over.

TO A FRIEND WITH A RELIGIOUS VOCATION

For C.

Thinking of your vocation, I am filled
With thoughts of my own lack of one. I see
Within myself no wish to breed or build
Or take the three vows ringed by poverty.
     And yet I have a sense,
Vague and inchoate, with no symmetry,
Of purpose. Is it merely a pretence,

A kind of scaffolding which I erect
Half out of fear, half out of laziness?
The fitful poems come but can't protect
The empty areas of loneliness
     You know what you must do,
So that mere breathing is a way to bless.
Dark nights, perhaps, but no grey days for you.

Your vows enfold you. I must make my own;
Now this, now that, each one empirical.
My poems move from feelings not yet known,
And when the poem is written I can feel
     A flash, a moment's peace.
The curtain will be drawn across your grille.
My silences are always enemies.

Yet with the same convictions that you have
(It is but your vocation that I lack),
I must, like you, believe in perfect love.
It is the dark, the dark that draws me back
     Into a chaos where
Vocations, visions fail, the will grows slack
And I am stunned by silence everywhere.

GREEK STATUES

These I have never touched but only looked at.
If you could say that stillness meant surrender
These are surrendered,
Yet their large audacious gestures signify surely
Remonstrance, reprisal? What have they left to lose
But the crumbling away by rain or time? Defiance
For them is a dignity, a declaration.

Odd how one wants to touch not simply stare,
To run one's finger over the flanks and arms,
Not to possess, rather to be possessed.
Bronze is bright to the eye but under the hands
Is cool and calming. Gods into silent metal:

To stone also, not to the palpable flesh.
Incarnations are elsewhere and more human,
Something concerning us; but these are other.
It is as if something infinite, remote
Permitted intrusion. It is as if these blind eyes
Exposed a landscape precious with grapes and olives:
And our probing hands move not to grasp but praise.

THE PRIDE OF LIFE: A ROMAN SETTING

Old men discourse upon wise topics here:
Children and women pass the shadows by,
Only the young are desperate. Their clear
And unambiguous gazes strike
Against each brushing hand or eye,
Their faces like

O something far away, maybe a cave
Where looks and actions always moved to hunt,
Where every gesture knew how to behave
And there was never space between
The easy having and the want.
I think the keen

Primitive stares that pierce this decorous street
Look in some far back mood and time to claim
A life beyond the urbane and effete
Where youth from coolest childhood came,
And look to look was like the hunter's throw—
Perpetually new and long ago.

MEN FISHING IN THE ARNO

I do not know what they are catching,
I only know that they stand there, leaning
A little like lovers, eager but not demanding,
Waiting and hoping for a catch, money,
A meal tomorrow but today, still there, steady.

And the river also moves as calmly
From the waterfall slipping to a place
A mind could match its thought with.
And above, the cypresses with cool gestures
Command the city, give it formality.

It is like this every day but more especially
On Sundays: every few yards you see a fisherman,
Each independent, none
Working with others and yet accepting
Others. From this one might, I think,

Build a whole way of living—men in their mazes
Of secret desires yet keeping a sense
Of order outwardly, hoping
Not too flamboyantly, satisfied with little
Yet not surprised should the river suddenly
Yield a hundredfold, every hunger appeased.

TWO DEATHS

It was only a film,
Perhaps I shall say later
Forgetting the story, left only
With bright images—the blazing dawn
Over the European ravaged plain,
And a white unsaddled horse, the only calm
Living creature. Will only such pictures remain?

Or shall I see
The shot boy running, running
Clutching the white sheet on the washing-line,
Looking at his own blood like a child
Who never saw blood before and feels defiled,
A boy dying without dignity
Yet brave still, trying to stop himself from falling
And screaming—his white girl waiting just out of calling?

I am ashamed
Not to have seen anyone dead,
Anyone I know I mean;
Odd that yesterday also
I saw a broken cat stretched on a path,
Not quite finished. Its gentle head
Showed one eye staring, mutely beseeching
Death, it seemed. All day
I have thought of death, of violence and death,
Of the blazing Polish light, of the cat's eye:
I am ashamed I have never seen anyone die.

ABOUT THESE THINGS

About these things I always shall be dumb.
Some wear their silences as more than dress,
As more than skin-deep. I bear mine like some

Scar that is hidden out of shamefulness.
I speak from depths I do not understand
Yet cannot find the words for this distress.

So much of power is put into my hand
When words come easily. I sense the way
People are charmed and pause; I seem to mend

Some hurt. Some healing seems to make them stay.
And yet within the power that I use
My wordless fears remain. Perhaps I say

In lucid verse the terrors that confuse
In conversation. Maybe I am dumb
Because if fears were spoken I would lose

The lovely languages I do not choose
More than the darknesses from which they come.

THE INSTRUMENTS

Only in our imaginations
The act is done, for you have spoken
Vows that can never now be broken.
I keep them too—with reservations;
Yet acts not done can still be taken
Away, like all completed passions.

But what can not be taken is
Satiety. Cool space lies near
Our bodies—a parenthesis
Between a pleasure and a fear.
Our loving is composed of this
Touching of strings to make sounds clear.

A touching, then a glancing off.
It is your vows that stretch between
Us like an instrument of love
Where only echoes intervene.
Yet these exchanges are enough
Since strings touched only are most keen.

REMEMBERING FIREWORKS

Always as if for the first time we watch
The fireworks as if no one had ever
Done this before, made shapes, signs,
Cut diamonds on air, sent up stars
Nameless, imperious. And in the falling
Of fire, the spent rocket, there is a kind
Of nostalgia as normally only attaches
To things long known and lost. Such an absence,
Such emptiness of sky the fireworks leave
After their festival. We, fumbling
For words of love, remember the rockets,
The spinning wheels, the sudden diamonds,
And say with delight 'Yes, like that, like that.'
Oh and the air is full of falling
Stars surrendered. We search for a sign.

SEQUENCE IN HOSPITAL

I. PAIN

At my wits' end
And all resources gone, I lie here,
All of my body tense to the touch of fear,
And my mind,

Muffled now as if the nerves
Refused any longer to let thoughts form,
Is no longer a safe retreat, a tidy home,
No longer serves

My body's demands or shields
With fine words, as it once would daily,
My storehouse of dread. Now, slowly,
My heart, hand, whole body yield

To fear. Bed, ward, window begin
To lose their solidity. Faces no longer
Look kind or needed; yet I still fight the stronger
Terror—oblivion—the needle thrusts in.

II. THE WARD

One with the photographs of grandchildren,
Another with discussion of disease,

Another with the memory of her garden,
Another with her marriage—all of these

Keep death at bay by building round their illness
A past they never honoured at the time.

The sun streams through the window, the earth heaves
Gently for this new season. Blossoms climb

Out on the healthy world where no one thinks
Of pain. Nor would these patients wish them to;

The great preservers here are little things—
The dream last night, a photograph, a view.

III. AFTER AN OPERATION

What to say first? I learnt I was afraid,
Not frightened in the way that I had been
When wide awake and well, I simply mean
Fear became absolute and I became
Subject to it; it beckoned, I obeyed.

Fear which before had been particular,
Attached to this or that scene, word, event,
Here became general. Past, future meant
Nothing. Only the present moment bore
This huge, vague fear, this wish for nothing more.

Yet life still stirred and nerves themselves became
Like shoots which hurt while growing, sensitive
To find not death but further ways to live.
And now I'm convalescent, fear can claim
No general power. Yet I am not the same.

IV. PATIENTS IN A PUBLIC WARD

Like children now, bed close to bed,
With flowers set up where toys would be
In real childhoods, secretly
We cherish each our own disease,
And when we talk we talk to please
Ourselves that still we are not dead.

All is kept safe—the healthy world
Held at a distance, on a rope.
Where human things like hate and hope
Persist. The world we know is full
Of things we need, unbeautiful
And yet desired—a glass to hold

And sip, a cube of ice, a pill
To help us sleep. Yet in this warm
And sealed-off nest, the least alarm
Speaks clear of death. Our fears grow wide;
There are no places left to hide
And no more peace in lying still.

V. THE VISITORS

They visit me and I attempt to keep
A social smile upon my face. Even here
Some ceremony is required, no deep
Relationship, simply a way to clear
    Emotion to one side; the fear
I felt last night is buried in drugged sleep.

They come and all their kindness makes me want
To cry (they say the sick weep easily).
When they have gone I shall be limp and faint,
My heart will thump and stumble crazily;
    Yet through my illness I can see
One wish stand clear no pain, no fear can taint.

Your absence has been stronger than all pain
And I am glad to find that when most weak
Always my mind returned to you again.
Through all the noisy nights when, harsh awake,
    I longed for day and light to break—
In that sick desert, you were life, were rain.

VI. HOSPITAL

Observe the hours which seem to stand
Between these beds and pause until
A shriek breaks through the time to show
That humankind is suffering still.

Observe the tall and shrivelled flowers,
So brave a moment to the glance.
The fevered eyes stare through the hours
And petals fall with soft foot-prints.

A world where silence has no hold
Except a tentative small grip.
Limp hands upon the blankets fold,
Minds from their bodies slowly slip.

Though death is never talked of here,
It is more palpable and felt—
Touching the cheek or in a tear—
By being present by default.

The muffled cries, the curtains drawn,
The flowers pale before they fall—
The world itself is here brought down
To what is suffering and small.

The huge philosophies depart,
Large words slink off, like faith, like love,
The thumping of the human heart
Is reassurance here enough.

Only one dreamer going back
To how he felt when he was well,
Weeps under pillows at his lack
But cannot tell, but cannot tell.

VII. FOR A WOMAN WITH A FATAL ILLNESS

The verdict has been given and you lie quietly
Beyond hope, hate, revenge, even self-pity.

You accept gratefully the gifts—flowers, fruit—
Clumsily offered now that your visitors too

Know you must certainly die in a matter of months,
They are dumb now, reduced only to gestures,

Helpless before your news, perhaps hating
You because you are the cause of their unease.

I, too, watching from my temporary corner,
Feel impotent and wish for something violent—

Whether as sympathy only, I am not sure—
But something at least to break the terrible tension.

Death has no right to come so quietly.

VIII. PATIENTS

Violence does not terrify.
Storms here would be a relief,
Lightning be a companion to grief.
It is the helplessness, the way they lie

Beyond hope, fear, love,
That makes me afraid. I would like to shout,
Crash my voice into the silence, flout
The passive suffering here. They move

Only in pain, their bodies no longer seem
Dependent on blood, muscle, bone.
It is as if air alone
Kept them alive, or else a mere whim

On the part of instrument, surgeon, nurse.
I too am one of them, but well enough
To long for some simple sign of life,
Or to imagine myself getting worse.

MAN IN A PARK

One lost in thought of what his life might mean
Sat in a park and watched the children play,
Did nothing, spoke to no one, but all day
Composed his life around the happy scene.

And when the sun went down and keepers came
To lock the gates, and all the voices were
Swept to a distance where no sounds could stir,
This man continued playing his odd game.

Thus, without protest, he went to the gate,
Heard the key turn and shut his eyes until
He felt that he had made the whole place still,
Being content simply to watch and wait.

So one can live, like patterns under glass,
And, like those patterns, not committing harm.
This man continued faithful to his calm,
Watching the children playing on the grass.

But what if someone else should also sit
Beside him on the bench and play the same
Watching and counting, self-preserving game,
Building a world with him no part of it?

If he is truthful to his vision he
Will let the dark intruder push him from
His place, and in the softly gathering gloom
Add one more note to his philosophy.

FATHER TO SON

I do not understand this child
Though we have lived together now
In the same house for years. I know
Nothing of him, so try to build
Up a relationship from how
He was when small. Yet have I killed

The seed I spent or sown it where
The land is his and none of mine?
We speak like strangers, there's no sign
Of understanding in the air.
This child is built to my design
Yet what he loves I cannot share.

Silence surrounds us. I would have
Him prodigal, returning to
His father's house, the home he knew,
Rather than see him make and move
His world. I would forgive him too,
Shaping from sorrow a new love.

Father and son, we both must live
On the same globe and the same land.
He speaks: I cannot understand
Myself, why anger grows from grief.
We each put out an empty hand,
Longing for something to forgive.

WARNING TO PARENTS

Save them from terror; do not let them see
The ghost behind the stairs, the hidden crime.
They will, no doubt, grow out of this in time
And be impervious as you and me.

Be sure there is a night-light close at hand;
The plot of that old film may well come back,
The ceiling, with its long, uneven crack,
May hint at things no child can understand.

You do all this and are surprised one day
When you discover how the child can gloat
On Belsen and on tortures—things remote
To him. You find it hard to watch him play

With thoughts like these, and find it harder still
To think back to the times when you also
Caught from the cruel past a childish glow
And felt along your veins the wish to kill.

Fears are more personal than we had guessed—
We only need ourselves; time does the rest.

ADMONITION

Watch carefully. These offer
Surprising statements, are not
Open to your proper doubt,
Will watch you while you suffer.

Sign nothing but let the vague
Slogans stand without your name.
Your indifference they claim
Though the issues seem so big.

Signing a paper puts off
Your responsibilities.
Trust rather your own distress
As in, say, matters of love.

Always behind you, judges
Will have something trite to say.
Let them know you want delay;
No star's smooth at its edges.

THE YOUNG ONES

They slip on to the bus, hair piled up high.
New styles each month, it seems to me. I look,
Not wanting to be seen, casting my eye
Above the unread pages of a book.

They are fifteen or so. When I was thus,
I huddled in school coats, my satchel hung
Lop-sided on my shoulder. Without fuss
These enter adolescence; being young

Seems good to them, a state we cannot reach,
No talk of 'awkward ages' now. I see
How childish gazes staring out of each
Unfinished face prove me incredibly

Old-fashioned. Yet at least I have the chance
To size up several stages—young yet old,
Doing the twist, mocking an 'old-time' dance:
So many ways to be unsure or bold.

A MENTAL HOSPITAL SITTING-ROOM

Utrillo on the wall. A nun is climbing
Steps in Montmartre. We patients sit below.
It does not seem a time for lucid rhyming;
Too much disturbs. It does not seem a time
When anything could fertilize or grow.

It is as if a scream were opened wide,
A mouth demanding everyone to listen.
Too many people cry, too many hide
And stare into themselves. I am afraid
There are no life-belts here on which to fasten.

The nun is climbing up those steps. The room
Shifts till the dust flies in between our eyes.
The only hope is visitors will come
And talk of other things than our disease . . .
So much is stagnant and yet nothing dies.

THE INTERROGATOR

He is always right.
However you prevaricate or question his motives,
Whatever you say to excuse yourself
He is always right.

He always has an answer;
It may be a question that hurts to hear.
It may be a sentence that makes you flinch.
He always has an answer.

He always knows best.
He can tell you why you disliked your father,
He can make your purest motive seem aggressive.
He always knows best.

He can always find words.
While you fumble to feel for your own position
Or stammer out words that are not quite accurate,
He can always find words.

And if you accuse him
He is glad you have lost your temper with him.
He can find the motive, give you a reason
If you accuse him.

And if you covered his mouth with your hand,
Pinned him down to his smooth desk chair,
You would be doing just what he wishes.
His silence would prove that he was right.

NIGHT SISTER

How is it possible not to grow hard,
To build a shell around yourself when you
Have to watch so much pain, and hear it too?
Many you see are puzzled, wounded; few
Are cheerful long. How can you not be scarred?

To view a birth or death seems natural,
But these locked doors, these sudden shouts and tears
Graze all the peaceful skies. A world of fears
Like the ghost-haunting of the owl appears.
And yet you love that stillness and that call.

You have a memory for everyone;
None is anonymous and so you cure
What few with such compassion could endure.
I never met a calling quite so pure.
My fears are silenced by the things you've done.

We have grown cynical and often miss
The perfect thing. Embarrassment also
Convinces us we cannot dare to show
Our sickness. But you listen and we know
That you can meet us in our own distress.

WORDS FROM TRAHERNE

'You cannot love too much, only in the wrong way.'

It seemed like love; there were so many ways
Of feeling, thinking, each quite separate.
Tempers would rise up in a sudden blaze,
Or someone coming twitch and shake the heart.

Simply, there was no calm. Fear often came
And intervened between the quick expression
Of honest movements or a kind of game.
I ran away at any chance of passion.

But not for long. Few can avoid emotion
So powerful, although it terrifies.
I trembled, yet I wanted that commotion
Learnt through the hand, the lips, the ears, the eyes.

Fear always stopped my every wish to give.
I opted out, broke hearts, but most of all
I broke my own. I would not let it live
Lest it should make me lose control and fall.

Now generosity, integrity,
Compassion too, are what make me exist,
Yet still I cannot come to terms or try,
Or even know, the knot I must untwist.

SAMUEL PALMER AND CHAGALL

You would have understood each other well
And proved to us how periods of art
Are less important than the personal
Worlds that each painter makes from mind and heart.

The greatest—Blake, Picasso—move about
In many worlds. You only have one small
Yet perfect place. In it, there is no doubt,
And no deception can exist at all.

Great qualities make such art possible,
A sense of TRUTH, integrity, a view
Of man that fits into a world that's whole,
Those moons, those marriages, that dark, that blue.

I feel a quiet in it all although
The subject and the scenes are always strange.
I think it is that order pushes through
Your images, and so you can arrange

And make the wildest, darkest dream serene;
Landscapes are like still-lives which somehow move,
The moon and sun shine out of the same scene—
Fantastic worlds but all are built from love.

ON A FRIEND'S RELAPSE AND RETURN
TO A MENTAL CLINIC

I had a feeling that you might come back,
And dreaded it.
You are a friend, your absence is a lack;
I mean now that

We do not meet outside the hospital:
You are too ill
And I, though free by day, cannot yet call
Myself quite well.

Because of all of this, it was a shock
To find that you
Were really bad, depressed, withdrawn from me
More than I knew.

You ask for me and sometimes I'm allowed
To go and sit
And gently talk to you—no noise too loud:
I'm glad of it.

You take my hand, say odd things, sometimes weep,
And I return
With rational talk until you fall asleep.
So much to learn

Here; there's no end either at second-hand
Or else within
Oneself, or both. I want to understand
But just begin

When something startling, wounding comes again.
Oh heal my friend.
There should be peace for gentle ones, not pain.
Bring her an end

Of suffering, or let us all protest
And realize
It is the good who often know joy least.
I fight against the size

And weight of such a realization, would
Prefer no answers trite
As this; but feeling that I've understood,
I can accept, not fight.

NIGHT GARDEN OF THE ASYLUM

An owl's call scrapes the stillness.
Curtains are barriers and behind them
The beds settle into neat rows.
Soon they'll be ruffled.

The garden knows nothing of illness.
Only it knows of the slow gleam
Of stars, the moon's distilling; it knows
Why the beds and lawns are levelled.

Then all is broken from its fullness.
A human cry cuts across a dream.
A wild hand squeezes an open rose.
We are in witchcraft, bedevilled.

A DEPRESSION

She left the room undusted, did not care
To hang a picture, even lay a book
On the small table. All her pain was there—
In absences. The furious window shook
With violent storms she had no power to share.

Her face was lined, her bones stood thinly out.
She spoke, it's true, but not as if it mattered;
She helped with washing-up and things like that.
Her face looked anguished when the china clattered.
Mostly she merely stared at us and sat.

And then one day quite suddenly she came
Back to the world where flowers and pictures grow
(We sensed that world though we were much the same
As her). She seemed to have the power to know
And care and treat the whole thing as a game.

But will it last? Those prints upon her walls,
Those stacks of books—will they soon disappear?
I do not know how a depression falls
Or why so many of us live in fear.
The cure, as much as the disease, appals.

GROVE HOUSE, IFFLEY

For Vivien

Your house is full of objects that I prize—
A marble hand, paperweights that uncurl,
Unfolding endlessly to red or blue.
Each way I look, some loved thing meets my eyes,
And you have used the light outside also;
The autumn gilds collections old and new.

And yet there is no sense of *objets d'art*,
Of rarities just valued for their worth.
The handsome objects here invite one's touch,
As well as sight. Without the human heart,
They'd have no value, would not say so much.
Something of death belongs to them—and birth.

Nor are they an escape for anyone.
Simply you've fashioned somewhere that can give
Not titillation, pleasure, but a sense
Of order and of being loved; you've done
What few can do who bear the scars and prints
Of wounds from which they've learnt a way to live.

CHINESE ART

You said you did not care for Chinese art
Because you could not tell what dynasties
A scroll or bowl came from. 'There is no heart'
You said, 'Where time's avoided consciously.'

I saw your point because I loved you then.
The willows and the horses and the birds
Seemed cold to me; each skilfully laid-on, thin
Phrase spoke like nothing but unpassionate words.

I understand now what those artists meant;
They did not care for style at all, or fashion.
It was eternity they tried to paint,
And timelessness, they thought, must lack all passion.

Odd that just when my feeling need for you
Has gone all wrong, I should discover this.
Yes, but I lack the sense of what is true
Within these wise old artists' skilfulness.

It would be easy now to close again
My heart against such hurt. Those willows show,
In one quick stroke, a lover feeling pain,
And birds escape fast as the brush-strokes go.

LOVE POEM

There is a shyness that we have
Only with those whom we most love.
Something it has to do also
With how we cannot bring to mind
A face whose every line we know.
O love is kind, O love is kind.

That there should still remain the first
Sweetness, also the later thirst—
This is why pain must play some part
In all true feelings that we find
And every shaking of the heart.
O love is kind, O love is kind.

And it is right that we should want
Discretion, secrecy, no hint
Of what we share. Love which cries out,
And wants the world to understand,
Is love that holds itself in doubt.
For love is quiet, and love is kind.

ONE FLESH

Lying apart now, each in a separate bed,
He with a book, keeping the light on late,
She like a girl dreaming of childhood,
All men elsewhere—it is as if they wait
Some new event: the book he holds unread,
Her eyes fixed on the shadows overhead.

Tossed up like flotsam from a former passion,
How cool they lie. They hardly ever touch,
Or if they do it is like a confession
Of having little feeling—or too much.
Chastity faces them, a destination
For which their whole lives were a preparation.

Strangely apart, yet strangely close together,
Silence between them like a thread to hold
And not wind in. And time itself's a feather
Touching them gently. Do they know they're old,
These two who are my father and my mother
Whose fire from which I came, has now grown cold?

THE ANIMALS' ARRIVAL

So they came
Grubbing, rooting, barking, sniffing,
Feeling for cold stars, for stone, for some hiding-place,
Loosed at last from heredity, able to eat
From any tree or from ground, merely mildly themselves,
And every movement was quick, was purposeful, was
                                                    proposed.
The galaxies gazed on, drawing in their distances.
The beasts breathed out warm on the air.

No one had come to make anything of this,
To move it, name it, shape it a symbol;
The huge creatures were their own depth, the hills
Lived lofty there, wanting no climber.
Murmur of birds came, rumble of underground beasts
And the otter swam deftly over the broad river.

There was silence too.
Plants grew in it, it wove itself, it spread, it enveloped
The evening as day-calls died and the universe hushed,
                                                    hushed.
A last bird flew, a first beast swam
And prey on prey
Released each other
(Nobody hunted at all):
They slept for the waiting day.

NEVER TO SEE

Never to see another evening now
With that quick openness, that sense of peace
That, any moment, childhood could allow.

Never to see the spring and smell the trees
Alone, with nothing asking to come in
And shake the mind, and break the hour of ease—

All this has gone since childhood began
To go and took with it those tears, that rage.
We can forget them now that we are men.

But what will comfort us in our old age?
The feeling little, or the thinking back
To when our hearts were their own privilege?

It will be nothing quiet, but the wreck
Of all we did not do will fill our lack
As the clocks hurry and we turn a page.

BONNARD

Colour of rooms. Pastel shades. Crowds. Torsos at ease in brilliant baths. And always, everywhere the light.

This is a way of creating the world again, of seeing differences, of piling shadow on shadow, of showing up distances, of bringing close, bringing close.

A way of furnishing too, of making yourself feel at home—and others. Pink, flame, coral, yellow, magenta—extreme colours for ordinary situations. This is a way to make a new world.

Then watch it. Let the colours dry, let the carpets collect a little dust. Let the walls peel gently, and people come, innocent, nude, eager for bed or bath.

They look newmade too, these bodies, newborn and innocent. Their flesh-tints fit the bright walls and floors and they take a bath as if entering the first stream, the first fountain.

A LETTER TO PETER LEVI

Reading your poems I am aware
Of translucencies, of birds hovering
Over estuaries, of glass being spun for huge domes.
I remember a walk when you showed me
A tablet to Burton who took his own life.
You seem close to fragility yet have
A steel-like strength. You help junkies,
You understand their language,
You show them the stars and soothe them.
You take near-suicides and talk to them,
You are on the strong side of life, yet also the brittle,
I think of blown glass sometimes but reject the simile.
Yet about your demeanour there is something frail,
The strength is within, won from simple things
Like swimming and walking.
Your pale face is like an ikon, yet
Any moment, any hour, you break to exuberance,
And then it is our world which is fragile:
You toss it like a juggler.

ANY POET'S EPITAPH

It does this, I suppose—protects
From the rough message, coarseness, grief,
From the sigh we would rather not hear too much,
And from our own brief gentleness too.

Poetry—builder, engraver, destroyer,
We invoke you because like us
You are the user of words; the beasts
But build, mate, destroy, and at last
Lie down to old age or simply sleep.

Coins, counters, Towers of Babel,
Mad words spoken in sickness too—
All are considered, refined, transformed,
On a crumpled page or a wakeful mind,
And stored and given back—and true.

CONSIDERATIONS

Some say they find it in the mind,
A reason why they should go on.
Others declare that they can find
The same in travel, art well done.

Still others seek in sex or love
A reciprocity, relief.
And few, far fewer daily, give
Themselves to God, a holy life.

But poetry must change and make
The world seem new in each design.
It asks much labour, much heartbreak,
Yet it can conquer in a line.

FIRST EVENING (from the French of Rimbaud)

She was half-undressed;
A few indiscreet trees
Threw out their shadows and displayed
Their leaves, cunningly and close.

She sat, half-naked in my chair,
She clasped her hands,
And her small feet shook
Where the floor bends.

I watched, on her lips
And also on her breast
A stray light flutter
And come to rest.

First it was her ankles I kissed;
She laughed gently, and then
Like a bird she sang
Again and again.

Her feet withdrew and,
In an odd contradiction
She said 'Stop, do.'
Love knows such affliction.

I kissed her eyes.
My lips trembled, so weak.
Then she opened her lips again and said,
'There are words I must speak.'

This was too much, too much.
I kissed her breast and, at once,
She was tender to my touch.
She did not withdraw or wince.

Her clothes had fallen aside,
But the great trees threw out their leaves.
I am still a stranger to love,
Yet this was one of my loves.

THE ROOKS (from the French of Rimbaud)

When the meadow is cold, Lord, and when
The Angelus is no longer heard,
I beg you to let it come,
This delightful kind of bird—
The rook—and here make its home.
One, many, sweep down from the skies.

Such an odd army—you birds.
You have very strange voices.
Cold winds attack your nests,
Yet come, I implore, as if words
Were your medium. Where the river rests,
Dry and yellow, by Crosses

And ditches, come forward, come
In your thousands, over dear France
Where many are still asleep.
This is truly your home.
Wheel over so that a chance
Traveller may see the deep

Meaning within you all.
Be those who show men their duty,
And also reveal the world's beauty.
You, all of you
(And I know this is true)
Are the dark attendants of a funeral.

You, saints of the sky,
Of the oak tree, of the lost mast,
Forget about those of the spring,
Bring back hope to the lost
Places, to those who feel nothing
But that defeat is life's cost.

FRIENDSHIP

Such love I cannot analyse;
It does not rest in lips or eyes,
Neither in kisses nor caress.
Partly, I know, it's gentleness

And understanding in one word
Or in brief letters. It's preserved
By trust and by respect and awe.
These are the words I'm feeling for.

Two people, yes, two lasting friends.
The giving comes, the taking ends.
There is no measure for such things.
For this all Nature slows and sings.

A SONNET

Run home all clichés, let the deep words come
However much they hurt and shock and bruise.
There is a suffering we can presume,
There is an anger, also, we can use;
There are no categories for what I know
Hunted by every touch on memory.
A postcard can produce a heartbreak blow
And sentiment comes seething when I see
A photograph, a Christmas card or some
Association with this loss, this death.
I must live through all this and with no home
But what he was, keep holding on to breath.
Once the stars shone within a sky I knew.
Now only darkness is my sky, my view.

LET THINGS ALONE

You have to learn it all over again,
The words, the sounds, almost the whole language
Because this is a time when words must be strict and new
Not concerning you,
Or only indirectly,
Concerning a pain
Learnt as most people some time or other learn it
With shock, then dark.

The flowers will refer to themselves always
But should not be loaded too much
With meaning from happier days.
They must remain themselves,
Dear to the touch.
The stars also
Must go on shining without what I now know.
And the sunset must simply glow.

HURT

They do not mean to hurt, I think,
People who wound and still go on
As if they had not seen the brink

Of tears they forced or even known
The wounding things. I'm thinking of
An incident. I brought to one,

My host, a present, small enough
But pretty and picked out with care.
I put it in her hands with love,

Saying it came from Russia; there
Lay my mistake. The politics
Each of us had, we did not share.

But I am not immune to lack
Like this in others; she just thrust
The present over, gave it back

Saying, 'I do not want it.' Must
We hurt each other in such ways?
This kind of thing is worse than Lust

And other Deadly Sins because
It's lack of charity. For this
Christ sweated blood, and on the Cross

When every nail was in its place,
Though God himself, he called as man
At the rejection. On his face

Among the sweat, there must have been
Within the greater pain, the one
A hurt child shows, the look we can

Detect and feel, swift but not gone,
Only moved deeper where the heart
Stores up all things that have been done

And, though forgiven, don't depart.